WATCHING THE POTOMAC BURN

POEMS BY CAROLYN SRYGLEY-MOORE

LUCHADOR PRESS

Luchador Press
Big Tuna, TX

Copyright © Carolyn Srygley-Moore, 2025

First Edition: 1 3 5 7 9 10 8 6 4 2

ISBN: 979-8-89975-015-1

LCCN: 2025940858

Acknowledgments:

I'd like to acknowledge my family
Of origin (mom, daddy, my brothers);
husband James & kid
Bynx; my wonderful publishers,
Especially Jason Ryberg & John
Burroughs —: each for their ongoing
Support. & my dogs & cats, for all
The love granted, steadfast.

A word for my employers since
1988, when I first entered the world
Of human services; each encounter,
Each client, made my inspiration
Greater, for the humor & determination
& resilience I see daily. Thank you.

Here's to freedom of expression—
The greatest fodder for
My tenacity as a patriot & poet.
I am happy to thrive still, though
My country is beset with
Conflict, as an older woman & artist.
      This is our fight —

TABLE OF CONTENTS

Winter 2024 - 25

Don't Restrain Me. / 1

Grounded. / 3

Dear Walter. / 5

Pink Eyeshadow Layered. / 8

Blasting Elton on that FM Radio. / 12

& I Saw a Gleaming Band of Horses. / 14

Reaching Twilight on Tiptoe. / 16

Angels of Laughter. / 18

For Charles G., Anthropologist, Curator, Friend. / 20

A Woman Rewrites the Reading. / 23

Solidarnos. / 26

January - April 2025

Tricksters of Boxcar Graffiti. / 31

Fathers. / 33

The Sound of Sunflowers. / 35

Refugee (Watching the Potomac Burn). / 37

Still Seeking Utopia in Real Time. / 41

A Quarter Century. / 43

Little Iron Lanterns Iron Ladies. / 44

The Necessity of Fuel. / 46

For "The Sisters of Mercy." / 49

Tai-Chi, 2025. / 50

Pigeon Shit at Mount Rushmore. / 52

Dear Darling. / 56

Spinning with Steinbeck. / 58

Blue Passport. / 61

Adventure some Poets Choose. / 66

Disappearances. / 68

Untitled. / 72

Perhaps We're Only Pretending. / 74

The Temporal Flux — Nostalgia. / 76

Wanting Brown Rice, Milk, & Honey. / 79

For the Gift of Nanna. / 81

Pink, the Starfish. / 83

You. / 86

Ode to the Messenger Pigeon. / 89

Passport Paul. / 90

What I Know I Do Not Know. / 93

Return to Sender. / 95

Nursery Rhyme Dragons. / 97

*"Cheerfulness and laughter despite — or no,
because of—Terror and pessimism."*

-Nietzsche

In memory of a wonderful member of the poetry
Community, & dear friend, Brian Fugette.

For Bynx.

Winter 2024 - 25

Don't Restrain Me.

You & I
Mount steps to
Mount the shine of archaeological
Quests
Defining that light
  Moon-halo
      We seek &
You believe (sometimes
I have such
Visions too)

6 miles away
Fixed & pulsating
Trickster astronomer
What is truth, Bethlehem? —. More

Than one chosen culture,
Darkness carves
  Many faces

The tree-ring center
The metro token
Totem
        Babe
& touching my chin
With your
Goatee & the ripe mouth hidden

You reached
Flooding my trees
With birds
Cresting

I can see
 Sutures disarming
     The anonymous wound

Grounded.

A guy strolled
Down the street with an acoustic guitar
    Which was odd for a
Village
(Sleepwalking)
Singing.
Curious
  So I watched
& on a corner of pale blue
  Snowbank drifts
        A
    Youthful guy knelt
& seemed to speak
Speechless to a woman,
Blue fringes
Of her Christmas shawl
    Shifted the wind.

When she said yes
(apparent from a distance)

I applauded
Birds flew from the trees
Like maple leaves

Darts

    Cherubs

Throw

  & the solstice sun recedes

Dear Walter.

Sleeping
You shift & turn,
Clutch a DVD,
A western,
  Tin of
Playing cards spilled
Over the bare floor,
  One king
Remains —:
John Wayne, his
Face a worn bookmark. Distance &
  Plastic
Tumbleweed season,
The lean of solstice here
& the gravel's dream, gasped
Tears a thin page of
"'what we know —"
(Your Navy baseball cap
  Like a psychic's top hat
Straddled by festive decorations)
 You mutter
The 3 Buffalo in Montana
(You describe the trail
Of spoor)
The core of your story —
  The moment in which
You read the memoir

You wrote —

Memory & feathers

What calls you from absence —

From gazing

Past the blue rock crevasse

Into the dark

Following nobody

& the massive hoof, up close,

Seems a gaudy

Thrift shop lamp base. I smile

You are sleeping,

An occasional errant sigh, &

I lay my ear to wall, smell

 Ammonia overwhelms

Like kidnapper's chloroform

Like the reek of cat pee.

  Yielding

Gentle the cadence enters &

I know the gallop of a zillion

Articulations

Muted, by any force —

What is your disorder,

  Your lithesome chaos —

What is your shine?

Sacred, this ; your fishing pole

Leaning in the corner

With a green tackle box &

The line lax trembles

Like a harpist's strum

& from a clearing

Dancers gowned oddly in leaves
Gesture
  "You don't get it"
"We know exactly what
We mean"

Pink Eyeshadow Layered.

1

Pink shadows
  Layered,
Marking our
  Faces
There's the voluptuous
Wind &
Solitude
Of youth
Eyes
  Mildly
Yelping, waiting
For something's reflection (if
Not the original) a tunnel
Damp underground train
Where futuristic monster rats nibble
Caviar
Of New Manhattan
Where
Causes are cargo, ballast & prop — yet
Picture books lean in our
  Window
Thing One
ThingTwo
  Banned
(Seuss cadences, wakes of river)
— yet carry —

2

How is it

An imaginary county
An arsonist's bible.
  Hollywood
Sign
    Eroding
 As do shorelines & mountains,
Cary Grant
& Grace
Only
  Superimposed
Hallucinations

& the service attendants
& pizza dough tossers
Sell potions
In a world of desire
So strange
So changed —

Like red roses
Suddenly purple as hyacinth
In the soup aisle

  & startled
  People

Sit at the potter's wheel
  Raise vases as a red clay spins
Glazed bright as elephant eyes
  Omniscient
        Utterly redeemed

3

How is it
The stink of lit
Sulphur
Evokes
Fireplace hearths of festival
Ghosting
The heartbeat
Over & over
Again?

4

Instinct
  Impulse

5

Offer a white-gloved hand — white
Satin just to
The elbow —
Set for the fabled Ball,
Twirling tango

As the lamp-houses
Wink
& on the knoll of
That
Bridge

The assassins
No longer stalk
No longer linger

& the goats play
 Nursing
    The new

Blasting Elton on that FM Radio.

Yes, mascara
Marking her face
 There's the voluptuous
 Blonde
Wiping red lipstick from her starry
 Teeth, lost
 Mildly
Yelping, waiting
 Perhaps
Homesick, maybe, bedded down
 In a metro
 Tunnel
Where monster rats nibble
Caviar
 Of New Manhattan
   Daddy's
Ringing
Civil war swords
& used bullets, oil
 Puddling
Moonlight
 Rainbows
   & it's an LA of laminate
& superimposed
Hallucinations
 & the service attendant
Sells love

A cardboard box red & white
 Stick fireplace
Matches
    & how is it
The stink of lit
 Sulphur
  Evokes
Fireplace hearths of festival
   Ghosting
The heartbeat
 Over & over
Again
  Juliet
      & Romeo
 Twirling tango
  As the lamp-houses
Wink
 & on the knoll of
That
Bridge
 The assassin
 & balding trolls
No longer stalk
No longer linger

(After the concept video for
"Tiny Dancer")

& I Saw a Gleaming Band of Horses.

The indigenous Americans built no walls
Running
Toward a river of horses
Like hands slipping epic
 Stories no
Longer told or known
Blind nocturnes pulsing
  Streaming moon & player
Keys, a rapt gleam
Cut from poached ivory;
  I can see the spaces
    Like wisdom teeth
      Cut & gouged & gutted
As the wakeful foals weep
Into the cadence
  A chorus, a choir of children
    & old
  People,
Wolves like us
The poets of watchtowers
  Dropping prison cliffs &
Singing tambourines
  The hooves a zillion galloping shoes
 (Clank the stake)
Cut from a zillion
Iron scythes
  Grafted from the body

Of wickedness & imagination
  Hinted
Of carnivals dizzily spinning
Vertiginous
  Melody
First came the calm
A pause
  From which all else
Reflects
  & proceed
Into a world of unnecessary walls

Reaching Twilight on Tiptoe.

Between dusk & night
Curtains
 Tore
Just as streetlights clicked
To yellow
Winks

Light cast & webbed blue
Marina windows — love
 Ghost-
  Crafted
 From shadow
As the horseshoe forms —: fuzzy eyed
The sensation, hazy

 Lucky jackrabbit foot keychains & string,
Bracelets sent
  Distances
Of wild salt & brine & languishing seal
   Populations now
Cornucopia

 Spilling birth & lifetimes braided
 Plaits
Bearing heat of the Bar Harbor rocks
  As a honeymoon
Whale too sang out:

"Dear
Water

     You are improbable to
Slay"
  & the shoreline prayed
 "Deep
     Draw deep
As the first inhale"
   "the pig
 Indeed
Was the first to fly
         Through the twilit
Animal
Barn"

The Angel of Laughter (After "Streets of
Philadelphia," Bruce Springsteen).

The road

   They say (pop
   Or greats of old rock n roll)

Is an impossible teaching :

Greyhound window cracked like the
Crease in a tulip petal
   Yellow
        Those old Manhattan cabs. Yet

As I write in blue ink
 The last line of a poem
"We love like pterodactyls "

You call like a biographer's stranger
   A sieve sensual, impulsive
Perched midst squall
    On a bell's gritty lip. Tonight

You say
  The future is my ghost
  As Dickens chants
& a flower seller does a back flip
 In a film

Eyes unique as a fingerprint
   Strike
         The sash &
As the lantern spins
Like heathcliff's tires

         A moth
      On route 100
At the loveless cafe
Alights & lingers, then flicks

Firework tongue of fried southern sausage
  The parking space
A drift of grey
A split squirrel or
  The ghost of a dog
            Trespassing the wake of
Route 100
   Red clay & tin cans & brush -/
Vanishing

         (The road)

      (Into a place where
Trees
   &
Children
Do not bleed)

For Charles G, Anthropologist,
Curator, Friend.

1

It's nearly like forgiving, this
Rubbing shoulders
In a different marketplace.
  Clarity —
 Fruits & vegetables, blue
Spruce, glass
Dragonflies
  Skimming lake ice.

No meat on the trading block
  Nothing of dulled or kidnapped
Spirits
  Crashing to rocks below

  "

It's nearly like forgetting
But shinier, a winsome gesture
Performed at some velvety
    Catacomb
Where hospital
Pediatric
    Cafeterias
Serve oxygen & sugar &
      Hot apple pie

& paper reindeer antlers
  & plastic dyed nativity
 & shining brass menorahs
   With baby dolls & toy red
        Cars

2

            Charles
The curator
   & global anthropologist
Excavated marvels from trench
& pit
    Where underground cataracts
Begin darling
Or

Venetian canals where
 Gondolas
Shift,
Pivot nearly ghastly
  A shade that inhales
        All timbre

  Midair
Like
        A sense of truth

    Glinting in the grit of pink-sand
On wing

The childlike
Paperback fantastically
  Imperfect
Gull.

(Christmas Eve)

A Woman Rewrites the Reading.

Juliet dismembers a jukebox
Turning screws with razor
    Filed
                Fingernails
    While reading poetry
At the Palais Royale
Those green dollar beers
Suited the palm

& —
        You — boy
Of streetlamp shadows -/:

        Did you begin to believe
Things the others
Hiss about skies
  Made of drops
        Fallen from first love's eyes;
Rumors
Webbed
Sticky
  Chaos, & who is that meteorologist
Mandating
        The world order?
    Each prisoner of
    Sedition & seduced

By troubadours
In blue raincoats
Singing aloud
From someone else's song.

Juliet,
Of a jungle's dark spirit
Eyes gleaming bright bright
  52 card pickup
Caste faces spilling face
Domino down,
    Those fun
Principles "of thermodynamics — that
Rebel
Mirrorgame." So says
    'The Philosopher
Queen
    From someone else's dream
      Calling-out the trickster:

(Tap the thimble
Covering the shifted pea)

"Where did that dome
Hiding the signal
go"
        "Is this the Death
Card
Or the twined nudes
Of True

Lovers "

"This choice
Is my last,   & it will be
My everything "

Solidarnos.

         Let us
       Get
The blue silk parachutes
& gather
A linked circle
Our togas dragging
In recall of the Parthenon
In Nashville
 Standing before Athena with
My mother
  When she was almost peace
    & wisdom

       Herself —

Sculptures stubbed
Arms, notched
Noses
From pilfering
Cultures
Dreams gathered like red
Pollen & dust
In the conduits
Where some arrogance
Tries
To reign in death
With designer watches &

Pacemakers
That grid our steps
Here,
  Stepping out upon a rope
Of smoke there

Like December children
  Craving travel &
Distant cities
Even to call
Out the poets &
  Riddlers — they who
      Animate the punchline
  As it tightropes
The carnival sky
 Where men look directly
      Into the eyes

& lie
3 times.

January - April 12, 2025

Tricksters of Boxcar Graffiti.

"The human all-too-human"..

-Nietzsche.

For a while
Carried
　　Like a blue jay feather
　You float
　　Over consequence
A canoe bumping dolphins mid-arc —

Even disrepair
An adventure
　Even poverty
　　Cigarettes & broiled chicken
Liver
25 cents a pound, Pakistani
Shop the corner
Of Calvert & 29th.

A stranger moves within the window
　Jangling tambourine
Bells　the hips of sunrise
Ring for the dancers, a gentle
Softshoe
　　　Along the edge of the city
Juggling boxcar
Freight eye &
Nightshade

Graffiti

Alive now,
Shuddering the wait of it
The weight of it
That birthmark puritan
That cannot be removed
"By salt by lemon, by light"
Without dire
Consequence
An electric train buzzing round & round
Crashing the stargazers
Disregarding the portents —
Maybe

Everywhere, a
Bourbon Street
Of New Year's Day

1/1/25

Fathers.

Like fire on a tongue of wind
  The ghost of a golden hound
          Trespassing the wake of Fairground
Avenue —

  &
Vanishing
  Within gaps, a midnight copse
      Of trees, exits gentle
Eased &
    Allowed

        Departure
Is an astonishing gasp
A rainbow oil glints in the driveway
That space
  Where a Cadillac heaped
With red & black
Geraniums
& orchids
  The twined threads
      Of root
Exposed
To
What warmth or chill
May advance
To the lives

Reveling in the greenhouse
Where elemental
Mercy
Reigns
Toy dolls
& Mr potato head

The sound of sunflowers

(For Jerry).

A flash

Electric fan blades
Cut &
 Whirr
Sea cresting
   Like the body
Sacred. Yet
            Some days
       As X discusses plastics
Of hustling
   /
        Of the hustled

            A flash

Beautiful
Jerry
     (We used to laugh a lot
   As we got lost
Serving banquet goose)
  A hotel
Waiter

He would weep into my hands

Then, shifting wings
   & tattoo charms
Stride
        Out to the Holiday Paradise

      Lot
Where men wait
  Wander
     Wonder
Amidst the exits
& foyers.

    "Hey where are you
       Jerry
          Honest as a razor"

The waxing
   Sickle
     Moon rises & hovers & drops
   Along the shaft of hope

     That sunflower
   Yellow bright bright
Dirt
  Stirs

      Flash

Gathers

Refuge: (Watching the Potomac Burn).

""But you are human !"
    He responds.

I've built this space
  Confection & strawberries
Crepe Suzette on Mother's Day
These fabulous dogs flying
   Red squirrel
         Nesting the treehouse —:
  The cadences the calm
    No cell block
On the ward / no
Block at the Y
        Yet enough
Of an island

Peace

1

    Today I woke up

Human, finally, no longer
  A subject
      Inhabiting another woman's room.

& when dusk drives apparitions

Of each love
That built cities within my clocks
& played ball with street kids
Kicking castes
Aside

Not

Engaging
The bullies'
Nonsense —

2

When cats & hutches
Fly across
The sickle moon as it wanes
Striking
Walls
Like cooked spaghetti —
Wall
Masonry taught
By the greatest teachers of the
Guild

You
Rushing the world
To restore

The world;
    Me
         Receding
As fear turned to
Giggles
  Spilling ink as I drew
What
We
Witness —
A wick of fire
Floating

3
  Outside storm windows
The coyote skirt &

    Great motherships
  Hover
Reading
The Morse of human sweat
Of bathing water, bubbling
  & pooling
     Drains

& spying upon myself
Spying upon you
Together
We

Stand tall

Calling-out the walls

As the orchards burn

Still Seeking Utopia in Real Time.

Everyone's talking dystopia
Zombies ripe in move theaters
Blue as Bane
Shooting up the witnesses
   As light flickers,
       One last cigarette
Found in a trench coat pocket
The tucked strings
Holding the gruesome mask.

     Listen
        On the car stereo

Simon & Garfunkel
   Working with enmity
  To manage harmony
Soaring out upon stretched fogs
&
Myths
    Of Central
Park

Once kind Rousseau came to Joplin
In a dream, handed her
 Spirits like firewood
In a bowl
Of iced saki shared from a

Utopian cooler:
Try to heal yourself Janis
    You are a world's voice
        Maybe the world

Will get better.

Hendrix nodding
Off
        Trancelike

        Dying young enough / old
Enough
    To have lain in beauty's bed,
    To have known her

As well as possible & glimpsed the
Calm
    Glinting
            When jackrabbits move
Amongst the rubble
With ghosts, sweet
        Ghosts; pirated
            Filaments
    & wisps,
 They
        have no need for
Gold

A Quarter Century.

"We loved one another
We loved one another
We had a good time "

My mother's words to me
A week before her death
 Though she didn't call me
By name anymore.

She knew who I was
When
 I called to check on her.

This marks the turn of a quarter
Century
    Let's Love
  Picnic

& be kind

Little Iron lantern Iron Ladies.

The villagers gather
    Packing the county fairgrounds
Where come July
We would take you under anxious
      Clouds or serene suns
To step upon
The paused spinning Ferris wheel —

"

      & tonight
Though it is
Winter
        &
The waterfront bells
Have stopped
Tolling
  I glimpse
     Brando in "Last Tango"
Turning
Midstream —:
      Light catches
A tear
Of grief's graffiti
 Jowls, coarse grey brush of them
The face
     An envelope
    Addressed only

To gargoyles guarding walkways
To inflatable men
& women,
  Lipstick pop &
     Graphic grotesquerie.
"

On some lawns
I recognize the lilt of things,
Wire
    Deer lit
   With white electric bulbs
Like petals, mammals
Fragile
As a rare white rhinoceros
   On unsteady
     Legs
& by that skeletal trace
A passage breaks
   My own darkness open.
I am not helpless
Chicken soup, snowfall
    An hour of SNL

The Necessity of Fuel.

Sitting still
With it, tracing
Bansky
Graffiti
On these dirty
  Stalker
Walls. Surely, I can ignore
Initials of lovers carved,
   Don't want to —

I can know
   We
Are
More
Than the stranger
       Immune yet
  Insatiably risk- bound.

In this glassy
    Spirit- jungle
Iris flash
A breach of trees
Scattering acorns
       Where
The dog walker
Taps his cane, echoes
    Bounce, deeper

Than the teal Caribbean waters.

       O seas

"I have chased monarch butterflies
In the Panama Canal

"Run out of fuel
& raised my orange life vest

"Toward
The given
Light

"As the darkness
Squirts inky
    Clouds
Like an octopus blinding
     The facts of water.

      "The night, also
    Plays dead
Plays rollover
Tickle my belly dog tricks

  "Some people burn wicks
Based in the manmade
Lake
      Of their cupped hands

"Catching sweet naive
Wind
   At its origin

"Swaying forward
The shark
      Hammerhead

"As it must
Move forward in order to live

For the "Sisters of Mercy."

Walkways are strange these days no sense, biting of
Eucalyptus or you painting in the attic

I wonder, sometimes if you are the girl in the story, my
Mother told when she would forget what year it was

    & honored when she called for me
By her puppy's name
"Marty

       "how old the tree in the greater sky?"
Certainly the hut
Planks had rotted

Once we moved
& certainly when I sat with you, as you sat with my
Mother, she told the story

Of the baby in the bassinet in the school in the river,
I remember
Nothing but the inland cataract, striking

The
Red of
Tennessee clay

Tai-chi 2025.

On a jungle gym bar
        A man hops
Right foot
Left foot
    Flashlight like bullets at his toes
  The Rockette NYC parades

Goddamn poets
    All of us, each
    "Can't find out who you are
By looking in the mirror"

The mask Grecian
Propped by kindling
  Thin—skinned
As an addict's memory

"Cannot sit here
    Waiting for
            A groomer a pimp an Epstein"
An adolescent says
Pulling at their yellow braid

        "Let's play soccer
    Walk on our hands
Paint our feet giggling
Walk over the bookcase"

Where Orwell quivers, delighted
     To see children pretending
To know nothing of the
Bomb

O mommy
   Dead mama
It feels
     Lonely now, another prairie,
Mountain sky seas.
Orange & red horizon
Sun dyed
& noosed

          Over the City of Angels
Someone's singing
Out loud
     Holding onto
  The porch railing

As Fire carries his room away
His blue glass rosary
His favorite chair,
   That one photograph.

Pigeon Shit at Mount Rushmore.

6 &
Trudging red cinnamon
Dust

Path along the river banks
I tagged after a crowd,
Kids

On the way to
The post. Mostly boys
Some girls ruffled pink

"They buried wild bunnies
& neighborhood
Cats alive"

& I / we
Knew the truth rumored
& I said nothing.

"

Someone told
Me
Years ago
As we sat amongst a field of ice
Sculptures

& Rushmore faces dropped stone
Like Greek feta crumbling

"The lanterns in my room
Are Broken
   Each night
Her dead babushka
Lights a white electric candle
Balanced
In our memories "

"

Smiling softly
(To be kind
To be gentle)

The purple bubblegum kitchen
The kitschy news
Anchors the evening

I stir stew peppered
With mirage

Taste it
Salty as split pea soup
My stomach lurches
A dirty gull midair

Crashing another bird

"

"Manson did nothing"
I laugh, the nonsense
Running
Viral
Into
My heavily aching lungs

"It's only a test" you say;
"The monsters are far"

"

Warm within this cave
Painted by native Americans
 We share herb
The teak hollow black
Gather resin

& the machines bleep
& drone

  Yellow-tailed
The cats & dogs
Scatter
Amidst the droppings

"

& deer give the sky a flash
A flicker

> Mammalian
> Milk
> Ephemeral

Are you
Only light

From a long dead star

Dear Darling.

Oases
Dripping

Darling

We shackle bad dreams
To free
   The shaved & shackled

         Intelligent
Elephants

   Washing caked mud
From their assaulted bodies
         Mouthy
Trunks stretching to feed
& water
The young

   Ash settles. My magnificent dead

Bear
   Bewildered & full of questions
"Why all
This blood
   & no oxygen?"

Assures me, it is time

Gather the dead

Glassy-eyed
Glazed

As Manson's
Sisters

Following command
As Charlie's
Hands
        Stayed clean

Rules of order —:

    The Tsar shot/

Yet mad Rasputin

The mob

    Tore
Limb
    From limb

Spinning with Steinbeck:

response to
'Of Monsters and Men."

I think of Red Pony
Spinning in the school rack
Of slim paperbacks,
Spinning like diner pies
 (The taste of lemon)

Reading
Of mice & —.

(*"Is fate always ruthless,"*
Said the given protagonist

     Embracing
Lenny, down by the river)

 Just
Crossroads
Where everyone pacts to sing
 Blood & spit
      With the shapeshifter.

At 11
I understood
 The protector's philosophy
Stay silent

& if the voice
Hiccups

Why the skull had to be
Crushed by a stone…

Id & ignorance
 Hands
Blind by misinterpretation
 Amongst
Actors
Numb as a battlefield medic
To pain

"I think of the many

Cats

Of Hemingway "

 I'm told
By men whose stories
Compel
Guesses within supper
Table silences—
 Grits & pickled
 Relish
 Southern ham
Pulse of ice
Clank

Cubes from the tray

In the Morse of wind talkers

"The cries all sound the same" /
   The cries
      Don't sound the same

Blue Passport.

Last night I saw you
Wrapped like licorice
Slipping
Through a tunnel

Of another woman's dream

I called your name
Anais snarled
On the red iron fire escape

"

We are silly
Lopping the drum sticks only

Sister & brothers
Playing chess
& wanting only to play
The rook's role
On a king's board

"

We wiggled

& this morning seeking

Youth before

The shit went down

We played
Butt naked
&
Understood

True at least
By the river's witness

  Red algae clung to
Our flesh
Intimate
As a birthmark

As irreparable.   Hawthorne
Murdered
By seeking perfection

(Perhaps make believe)

2

& the woman at the hearing
Place

 Eyes large as the orbs
Of Poe's women

Veiled
As is custom
In mesh lace of St Valentine
A corner bridal shop
In Troy
By the door factory
Each gown
Half price

Give
Me a large key
To everlasting sensibilities
Even as my eyes
&
My ears

Sink in purpose

3

& maybe we'll all fall asleep
At once

Our festival seasons
&
Ritual
Nodding into
Narcoleptic numb

or maybe
Rise
Like that
Man overseas
Clamoring

By incident
By accident

 Set afire

Grotesque

Lips mouthing the mana

Of gratitude

What
Else remains

4

 Uncanny
A silhouette
Orange
& red
A blackboard background
 Seeking
    Dignity as

Like a wolf's lamb

He flickers
 A droplet
        Of rain
"Have you seen the wonder"

Water &

Purpose undone

5

There is nuance
To a puppy's whimper
Curled in a teacup or on death row; nuance

To the mind
Expanding contracting electromagnetism
That alters heat & cold
Simply when
It says hello

An Adventure Some Poets Choose.

You were just a boy
(Timeless)

A kid - gentle —
I found
In the mountains

Whimsy
Flit flit
Amongst the leaves

Of monsters & dragons
Damp licked tame displaced
By night

         & an ice cream
"Bo, it's really
    Sticky on my fingers"
I didn't think to use my tongue

What did I know
Of love

What did I know
Of pleasure

    I was just a girl — a kid, gentle —

Frocked in flowers
Stupid & careless

I can't help
But cuss flaying tongue
Like an imposter no imposter at all;
    No regrets,

How you nudged my heart
With your grief

Your storm the storm
Of a stowaway
The honey cantinas of Manitou

& does it matter
Your intent?

I was a girl

Danger my mentor

My ponytail
By curiosity
Undone

Disappearances.

Once Carla said
"Please don't go,
I'm frightened,"

Like April muttered
The other day
Under a cloud of breath

"Don't leave me."
It's honest anyway; no flailing

About in the fog
Misinterpreting & thinking a kiss
      Makes us relevant.

"It's all they want."
The mothers & grandmothers
Talked the forecast
Each morning
As in a daze

Everyone loved
Falling
Away

"We respected you,"
 Said Alex

" we would have protected you ."

 Did I say it out loud
  "Don't leave me —" —
        Shout out to
Father..

Sit with it babe
I'm talking to you
Sitting in the red footbridge
0
Pennsylvania
Our legs swinging
You, the little girl
That
    Like oxygen borne
On a red blood cell
Has become
Me.

We are at one.

"

Isn't that what it means
My masters
Of B movie monsters

When you retreat
Seeking

Self defense —

"You
Must protect yourself " said Jane.

Each night
Daddy knew Demons
Of war

Flashback
Electrocution—
He saw that woman
In black
At
The carrier
Bow; me,

I saw a radio thrown in the bathtub
A body taut
Last words
A cognition of what is frivolous
Trivial

People
Disappear

The river-bloat of the kidnapped teen
& Elvis Costello singing

What is absurd about death these days

Is that Regina Spector bells are

Faint as the stars

Where the skies of Galileo

Allowed a vista

Seurat

So crowded with pinpricks white

Like a string of lights

Crackling

Popcorn

              In the movie

Yes
But the
Movie was real

The arson, real

Untitled.

We may be circus
Freaks, on that line circling
Like silly cats on bicycles. Maybe not —.

I'm considering that gentleman

Kiev Beirut Gaza Jerusalem
Some think he's freaking
Out
The compass spinning
But he's
No freak

Texting the journalist as bombs
Gut & change stone to ether.
"Bless…".

Ah, this is flowery (too much/
Enough? Or need I //
Or should I be raw? It's dark

& ink has a certain poverty
The wind, fierce.

The dogs stir.
I hear him speak
To me in translation—//

Stardust wind is breath
A zillion angels carry

& love poems are written everywhere
 Even
As the palm flashes
& the hare of terror disappears

Perhaps We're Only Pretending.

Or it's the humor of deities, these
  Mosaic
Clouds unthreading,
Nooses unknot — once

  You said
  "Drama queens & divas die off
Early". Headed downtown

  While — discussing the forecast —
The old ones quip
"It's no fuss" & endure , bussed
      Past
          That iron bench
Fixed upon any overpass or classic crossroads
Where the poet exchanges
Their own soul
            To write & draw
A truth.
      You,
The comedian; yet
From home interstellar
After hour
    Dialogues
          We talked happily about
How pink the brain
Seems

Full of quivering
    Always
        In the process
    Of dying
Of being born

The Temporal Flux — Nostalgia.

The squeals
                    Enchant
Me, I don't know what froth
This is, mouthing

Rage &

It's nostalgic now.
Zombies eat children's plump hearts
For breakfast

It's everywhere (you pretend
 You can't see it, you drink
Because you can see it)

 Conveying
What dignity is (would you leave
A dog at the side of the road ?).

A boy just died in Africa
Because those with no soul speak

"Birds that are robot spies " — grown men
Casting automobiles across
The television screen

Stages cut of cardboard
Soggy with elements
A step out
        Upon no floor
            Upon no floor

"

        Dear the Psalmist

    The hypocrite taints

"

"& it is always the Other
  Who is not chosen:
    Until you are the mother

    & your baby has no
Medicine

"Your baby has no medicine"
Nanna sings

Lightly
 Words float
Like sea foam
A calculation
Of what is
Immeasurable

Both love & absence

I *miss you*
I *miss you more*

"

       Rants, love love
Soothsayers &
Oracles
       By the cinnamon
Girl
River. That's what got you — floating

   The other way
One step on the greyhound
& even that
       Dog Star
We looked
Toward
       When lovers
Everything new & winter
Gnawing gently at our faces

"

The knock at the door
The knock at the door

Wanting Brown Rice, Milk, & Honey.

I want to be seen
But in the shimmy of a moment
        Only a flash
    & the flapper's sequined sash,

Quick quick

Forgotten ;
Only an imprint, a thumb,
        Bald from acid

Burning the whorls — anonymous,
My names & nicknames
        What I become in another's mouth

In your blank card
In the journal flashlights compose;

In dad's last exhale
Body pressed to prairies of sky,
        Flesh & jungle,

Warmth, reaching, flight
No longer the gull of
Heart-void on wings.

        Dropped bombs can't

Strike the core
(The translucent translation)
    Cut from
The peach stone whittled
    Anchors &

Actors

Stage front
& center.

A singer — Torres — says she likes
"To be seen" — bold, not hesitant.
    Others
Still duck
Like a baby or
        The wiggly puppy
Peekaboo
        Peekaboo

Waiting for the machinations, Sci-fi
That future —
    Metronome click click —
The future
        The one, broken brain saxophone
Blue

                Already arrived

For the Gift of Nanna.

The trees, Black Forest fairytale
You write
Down in an alphabet not your own.

Shaggy
  Weeds within
            Tentacular & your heart
Stops
Writhing.

              Happily

The red foxes approach
    You as you lean
From an urban window

("The geology
All a-jumble")

The sky graphic smudged
  Conjured & summoned
Down,
The feral heat of Death Valley

("At night
    The flamethrower approaches—")

I hear you laugh
Like froth sea foam bioluminescent

Liquid light,
A kitchen scene
("Close the damn window would you -/")

Where Williams plays himself
The comic the poet
The soul at the Groom's right hand

Balanced gestures on the stern of
Methuselah, rays omniscient
The oldest of

Known

Stars

Pink, the Starfish.

Authentic
As chocolate kisses
The kitchen table & hutches
  Disappeared into
        The banana moon's grim smile,
Boomeranged ("karma,"
Said Sharon,) crashing
The walkways & walls
   We'd known as sweet jungles
            & concrete waterfalls.

Damn, I want this memory

Even if
The details of the leaf

Or the shadows of her hands
As they gesture
Passionately
About the Nile
Knowing Atlantis —
The place Plato recovered —
Shadows
      Dark
   As tangling seaweed

  Uncomfortably

"

I want to remember every detail

I need to understand the monster
    Within / outside —

("What's that?
            That reflection in my mirror?") ("I see
Nothing where you see
Me.")

"

Even
                That One
To whom I chose obedience
Even as Rimbaud opened his pages
In a heap
In the 29th street book house floor

& comforted.

For even disorder is sacred:

The hutch regenerates
    A pink starfish
& all things of childhood
& things of home or the river

Light Broken
   Are just orange & black
  Worms
Migrating
           Into a metamorphosis
Even monsters
("You must've done many
Bad things in your life " said
Sharon.)
                Curiously

Comprehend

& if I remember

I know to sit with
It,
Peeling
A
Boiled
Egg
Husking
Corn
The silk of coming summer

You.

Heard weeping
  Sand grinding
Anything fresh & alive
To hell

  An intersection somewhere
Avenues or
Corridors above hospital bridges

Where they wheel
Stranded
People
    Locked & gagged
Not knowing love
Trained, nurtured.

 I too was walled
Godzilla's
Nemesis & even

   I brushed your fear aside.   Rough, no
I was a fraud really, baby
    Not a bad girl —
So much in love with the world
  I floated
          In solitude

"

& maybe I'm a grenade these days
Sweetheart
A watchdog
At the watchtower

   A

Silent

Lion.

      Saw a lady on West Avenue

Riding a hot pink trail bike
 Deep black
Hair unkempt
In helmet of beautiful
Defiance
Irreverence
Absurdity

  Riding into the sunrise

      "Go east —"

& all I can feel

Is that I am

Crowded

An auditorium

Buried

In my microphone

Stranded

That red sandbar

An island to some
          Glimpsed
    Across
The Strait
      Of Gibraltar

  Seafarers

Know

The galaxy
To another

Ode to the Messenger Pigeon.

Paring the golden pears (Galileo or Newton?)
From the wire umbrella tree
  Like a starfish
     Each arm to regenerate
& pile in a judge's brass scale
From which grey pigeons lift
        Paper messages
Carrying them across tariffed boundaries
As love takes agency — thwarts
                Unmasking masked
Figures
Who rattle the poacher's shackles
     & handcuffs
Bearing down on
Sisters
            & brothers. Eagerly
In real time they wave for a yellow chariot
Borrowed from a culture's
    Muttered
Declination— ah, lovers ours

    Homeless as the punchlines
The last laugh
The last word
  Thought but left unspoken

Passport Paul.

     A gargantuan black
Cat, face blank
For velvet imaginings
(The Sphinx's missing nose);

The piano abandoned
 Rocking the bassinet
Rocking palms
 Impregnated wings
Flying the sea, friend

That lean composer, Paul,
Arterials blue &
Mauve
 Tracing the muscles, jaguar
Steady & sure

As he said
"Lean into the instrument " — sway
  Push
Embrace
 The metronome -

Forget yourself
While

Using
  The core of each inhale
  The science & mythic
        Johnny Appleseed

All & every possibility
Each sacred exhale
Like eyes
  The disorder
    The disruptive reef of Vision

Forget—:
That you may know the natural lake
  The pure lack, the solar purr
Floating on your back
  Paddling
The cornucopia wake of

Hope
& consequence
  As the monarch wisely
  In its uncanny camouflage
Steadies its wings
Headed south away
  From these wintry tanks & bells

    Passport & suitcase &
Piano

Packed

  Including

That orange lipstick (1973)

That you

      like

Because it speaks & dazzles

What I Know I Do Not know.

Rip Van
Winkle slept in the Catskills
I learned from the lady in warship black
At 14
Sparrow Avenue , an alley downtown.
"Any native New Yorker knows that ."

  Coming back from the bar
You laughed out the car window
& the hound wagged her
Tongue
   At the valley of hunters

We drove through those snowy crags
& hushed sirens, counting
Army envoys heaped
 With galaxies
     Hands & North Stars

Vaping to dull how
Visceral
 Bouncing molecular
Blood hissing in our code
Blue wrists

The memory
Of sleeping, embraced by octopus arms —.

After the people dismantled
Who I was ; floating
Easily
On the blood rafts of your self/portrait
The carpet feathers

Floated with limbs. Head on a stick. Dolls
Easily fell apart — little hooks
& stories of red rubber bands—
You know
The game. Paper beats stone

Scissors
Beat paper
But messenger pigeons
  Bearing flags like love

 Letters smeared in the rain
Gain legibility by salt & sun

Return to Sender.

Maybe desire is the world's fiercest
Lament & most primal
     Ebullience
  Skin's texture rough with
Frost's teeth, sheer
Water &
Cream
       Breaking dawn's

Snow & maybe we indolently
Laughed
    Turning our bodies
Like wild
Boars on a stick
Over
     & over

A burning pyre upon which
Love letters wrap
  Seaweed
Around rib cages
Trembling
 Canary tips within
   Rooting

My laugh & yes
We behaved

Badly
Wasting your time
Urging your fears
Under
  The ceiling

Mirror
Where I could see the letters
 Salvaged from
Underwater
Brine
&

   Feathery gills

By which both of us could
At last
        Give
Our faces back to the gorilla
Mirror, silverback &
Shined like a
   Slipper —

Then returned
To ourselves

Nursery Rhyme Dragons.

Gravity facts & solace
The weight of you

Safe
  Upon me
        Each pulsing where blood knows
            Itself, its purpose,
Under
            Intent sweet
Sweet

——-

Maybe its images floating
With alligators in the bayou

    How above
        Hovering

Helicopters
Cut & cut

———

O fairy tales.
  Taught me good

Fist was laughter
A blue jay feather
Striated pink with sunrise —

Allen said it.
At the ice cream shop
Spelling out
        The 1st step —

"You think
Cruelty is a joke at first." He
 Covered
His mouth, coughed.   Long term Covid
—:

"In time
You open your mouth find speech
 Within her heat

 "Intime its void."

"

Dammit

When your watering hole
When your utopia

Is my nightmare

Nursery rhyme dragons

—

Everywhere & anywhere
Kicking can in the alley
(Yeats said it way
    Better & full of lanterns)

Just a mother
Calling out
  "It's dark
  There are strangers about"

 The fish tank in grandfather's house
A pink fish shaped like a cerebellum
  (sister called him Brain) .

——

    You open a stout
Filled the room with scent
  Like a 3 wick candle
Flat as the earth
    I've never recognized
Full of robot women
Whining
About
Fallen chess pie meringue

We feed like hummingbirds
& how swift
   & full of pause
When nectar strikes fuselage
& belfries
     In the blood

"

Allen glimpsed pea green tanks on the margin

Where people burn
Flares

    & sand luminaries
        Trace the banks of

Someone's backyard creek

    Water fresher than
        The Hudson

Babies sputter like toy engines

Going uphill

Forever uphill

A long ago graduate of Johns Hopkins Writing
Seminars & a student of the masters program,
SUNY-Albany: Srygley Moore Carolyn, since 2009,
has written books to include: *Miracles of the BLog*:
a series (/2012), poetry & visual art; *Enough Light
on The Dogwood* (mimesis press, 2009, online)
Reading Backwards Through the Yellow (Writing
Nights Press). *Ode to Horatio and Other Saviors*),

was released at the onset of Covid (Crisis Chronicles Press). *For All of my Beautiful Ghosts,* & *Laying Flowers along the Boundary* (Posthuman Poetry & Prose.) were in the same period as were *Termites amidst The Milky Way* & *Parking lot Poems* (Kung Fu Treachery Press). All collections are interesting collaborations with great publishers. Most ofthe book covers are her original art & photographs.

October 2025 — we are excited to share with you guys *Watching The Potomac Burn* (Luchador Press,) (Photos). Maybe authenticity can prevail in the current world, maybe fact & kindness will prove triumphant over the current chaos & cruelty & dissolution of human rights & autonomy. It is a global phenomenon, but the Potomac marks the White House. Srygley-Moore won 2 Kenan Awards for poetry at Hopkins; 2 pushcart nominations 1 best of the web.

This project was made possible, in part, by generous support from the Osage Arts Community.

Osage Arts Community provides temporary time, space and support for the creation of new artistic works in a retreat format, serving creative people of all kinds — visual artists, composers, poets, fiction and nonfiction writers. Located on a 152-acre farm in an isolated rural mountainside setting in Central Missouri and bordered by ¾ of a mile of the Gasconade River, OAC provides residencies to those working alone, as well as welcoming collaborative teams, offering living space and workspace in a country environment to emerging and mid-career artists. For more information, visit us at www.osageac.org

Osage Arts Community